Russell Wilson

The Life Story of One of the World's Greatest Football Players

By Jayson Morris

Table of Contents

Introduction

American football star, Russell Wilson, has come a long way. He fought all disbeliefs about his small stature and quickly moved up the ranks to become one of the elite athletes in his sport.

Much of his giftedness in athletics comes from his family. His grandfather was a two-sport athlete at Kentucky State University, and his father had great prospects in an NFL career before he turned to law and prepared his son for a life of greatness in sports.

Despite his huge success, Russell stays a kind, down to earth human being. He inspires millions of people through his actions and he is a role model for a large amount of young people. He has lived a life less ordinary, defying all skepticism about his height. Russell believes that he is 5'11" for a reason. He believes that it was to set an example in front of the world that a person of his size could be one of the best in the sport of football, which is almost exclusively full of very tall people. And it's not just about his height. He maintains that through his example, all such children who have been told they can't achieve something will feel inspired and push themselves harder.

In the course of this book, we will learn about the life and achievements of the American football star, Russell Wilson, and how he became the enigma that he is today. I thank you for choosing this book and hope you have fun reading it.

Chapter 1: The Birth of a Star

"Potential just means you haven't done it yet. Already in my career, I've seen that lots of people have potential, but not everyone does it."

Russell Wilson

Russell Carrington Wilson was born to Harrison Benjamin Wilson III and Tammy Wilson, on November 29, 1988, in Cincinnati, Ohio. He has two siblings; elder brother, Harrison IV and younger sister, Anna. Later, his family would move to Richmond, Virginia where he grew up. Russell was an active kid, and was particularly interested in sports from a very early age. His grandfather, Harrison B. Wilson Jr., saw in him the potential to be a great athlete. He saw the child swing a baseball bat and somehow knew that Russell carried the legacy of his family with a history in sports. Harrison, Wilson's father, was a star athlete at Dartmouth in both baseball and football.

Russell was introduced to football at the age of four, which he played with his father and brother. As expected, little Russell developed a liking for the sport. He would also go on to play baseball and basketball. Early in the morning before school, Russell used to play catch with his father. Sports eventually became something he thoroughly enjoyed, and he tried to spend as much time as possible playing sports. He wasn't very keen on studying and he was lucky to have siblings who also loved sports. His sister is currently an accomplished basketball prospect. His brother also played football in high school. Having played against Harry, Russell always had to push his limits. That is where he learned to love the game and developed the will to work harder every time. It could be said that his predisposition to become a successful quarterback was the way he practiced with his brother, who was a receiver. He really did get a lot of practice, and is now one of the best at throwing a football.

As a three-year-old, Russell remembers thinking, "I could be something special one day." Well, why not? He received praise from almost everyone. He would be told how they thought he was poised to be great; how he could be a pro athlete. The overconfidence would have gotten to Russell's head, had it not been for his father. Harrison kept him grounded. He said, "Son, potential just means you haven't done it yet." It is something that helped Russell not let the success go to his head. He believes that it is not the moments when "life tells you yes" which define you. It is the ones where you are denied what you think you deserve. It is that same feeling, which keeps Russell motivated in the worst of times.

Chapter 2: Growing Up

"My dad used to wake me up at 5:30 in the morning and hit me ground balls and tell me, 'don't be afraid to excel. Don't be afraid to be great.'"

Russell Wilson

Harrison was a disciplined and strong individual, and he truly influenced Russell's life the most. "He taught Russell work ethic and discipline," claims Russell's mother. He would train his son and teach him morals. He raised all of his children to be spiritual. It is because of this that Russell has high self-worth and always stays motivated.

One of Russell's best qualities is that he believes in himself. He says, "I have high expectations of myself. I always have, always will. That will never waver. I always believe in my talent - always have." His father instilled in him a competitive spirit, to never settle, to keep on going further and further.

He was taught that there is always space for improvement.

Those who know Russell and his father would vouch for one thing; that Russell is an embodiment of his father. There are similarities in the physical appearance, notably. However, it also seems that he carries his father's temperament and shares the same beliefs as his father. For Russell, no compliment would be greater. He looked up to his father and growing up to personify his life would be the way to go. It is interesting to note that in contrast to all the similarities, he did not share his father's flair for studying. Russell's parents made sure that he took care of his academic progress alongside his athletics.

"I used to beat up kids and bite kids and do stuff all the time," admits Russell. The nature of humans is such that some are more assertive and command authority effortlessly, and such was the case with him. He used to direct other kids in the class as a fourth grader. "I think he was a leader then," says his mother. Harry calls his brothers claim of being a 'bully' quite a bit of an exaggeration. It is inconsequential whether we can ascertain the validity of such statements, but one thing is clear; Russell has great leadership abilities as evident from his shining career as a pro quarterback.

It would not be fair to discuss Russell's childhood without mentioning the Seattle Supersonics. Like all other kids at that time, Russell thoroughly enjoyed video games. "When I was about eight or nine years old, my older brother Harry, and I would battle in NBA Jam on the Super Nintendo in our bedroom almost every day," he says. That was where he became a fan of the Seattle Supersonics. He followed the team and never missed watching them whenever he had the chance. Russell loved their name. He loved the green on their uniforms. Russell talks about it further, saying, "I loved Kemp and Payton, and then in later years, I loved watching Ray Allen swish corner threes with that perfect form."

Russell knew he was good at sports. He knew something needed to be done about his performance in academics. It wasn't much of a surprise that he did not like school much. Young as he was, one could clearly see that his life was about sports.

If you were to ask his mother, she would say he only liked the socialization at school. He was always friendly and would try to get to know the other children. He knew that there were others who performed better than him at academics. The ones he knew were 'smarter' than him. He soon realized that he could receive some help by helping his friends at things he does better - sports. Since the smart boys in his class weren't excelling at sports, he would make them practice. They would learn the sport from him, and in return, they gladly agreed to help Russell with his academics. This little arrangement reflected his personality; he wanted his friends to improve and they would assist him in his desire to do better at his studies. He truly believes that one can achieve more if they keep working towards it.

Russell's positive outlook was brought on by his upbringing. He, being the younger one, could not beat his brother at sports. Most people would consider giving up if that was the case. But Russell did not know or experience giving up. His positivity cultivated a habit of persevering. He would try with all his might every time he played with his brother, only to end up losing. He would never let this get to him, and he never ceased to stop trying. Sometimes he would run to his mother telling her how Harry dominated him. "If you can't handle it, then maybe you need to stay inside," his mother used to tell him. Unrelenting as he was, Russell would shake it all off and go back to playing with his brother. It would be fair to say that this repeated exercise of making an effort each time he lost to his brother polished his sportsmanship. It made him tough, his mother remarks.

Chapter 3: School and the Start of a Sports Career

"I truly believe in positive synergy, that your positive mindset gives you a more hopeful outlook, and belief that you can do something great means you will do something great."

Russell Wilson

Harrison always supported his boys and trained them not only in sports, but also taught them good manners and how to present themselves as athletes. He would tell them how to talk about sports as professional players do. He motivated them to achieve more. He believed that they had the capability to be elite players, so much so that he would make them practice acceptance speeches in case they ever won the Super Bowl.

By the time he was seven, Russell was facing fake press conferences his father arranged to make him more careful with what he said and did. He showed his son that his actions and behavior are of the utmost importance. He was training him to be well behaved, with the right attitude that would lead him to success. His father's work bore fruit, as it is a well-known fact that Russell is a thorough gentleman. He is never heard saying something wrong or inappropriate.

An ambitious child, Russell worked hard day and night, honing his athletic skills. He had the will to be a professional athlete and had the perseverance and hard work to back it up. By high school, he knew he wanted to be a two-sport star, to play both football and baseball professionally. He attended Collegiate School at Richmond. His elder brother also played for the Cougars, the Collegiate School football team. Russell was a ball boy at that time, in about eighth grade. He would throw the ball as the referee asked for it, and the spectators would see the ball fly through the air. His arm was phenomenal for his age.

He knew he could throw well and he had speed; he wanted to play as the starting quarterback for his school. Seeing the history of successful quarterbacks, one would quickly notice the one thing they all had in common. They were really tall and well built. Even so, Russell faced the doubt from onlookers that he might not actually be able to be a good quarterback after all. But he had faith in himself. He began practicing even harder, giving it all he had. He knew himself and had full confidence that he could make it.

Russell started improving his game each day. He had his eyes on his target and he wanted to make sure that he won when he got the chance. He practiced his passing and trained to be faster. Days went by and he trained rigorously without breaking a sweat. All through his freshman year, he only had one goal. He could see himself playing as the starting quarterback for the team. Soon, it would be time to put his skills to the test. Was he good enough to make it?

Chapter 4: High School

"I had this urge to play the game of football, because so many people - I shouldn't say so many, a handful of people - said I couldn't do it. For me, it was one of those things that I just believe in my talent that the Lord gave me, and I wanted to take advantage of it."

Russell Wilson

It was time for Russell to prove himself. He was in tenth grade, his sophomore year. He was to compete for the position of the starting quarterback. The day of the trials, he got out his bed with excitement. He felt that he was ready. That day, he would go on to show the results of his hard work. Russell's performance exceeded all expectations. It seemed as if nothing could stop him from achieving what he had in mind for himself. He could see himself getting closer and closer to his goal as the time passed. He was in high spirits. But when do things happen exactly as we expect them? It had been apparent that Russell would make a fine quarterback, but wouldn't be able to be the starting quarterback for this team after all. What was the reason? It wasn't the lack of effort on Russell's side. There was someone just as good as him.

As it turned out, a junior year student, an eleventh-grade student who stood 6'5" tall had about the same odds at the starting quarterback as Russell had. It all came down to the head coach Charles McFall. He was supposed to make the decision about the selection. Who would he pick? Russell had his dream right in front of him. And there he was, waiting for someone to decide whether he had reached his goal. Months of training and someone else gets to decide; so Russell started getting anxious. Interestingly, the coach had something better in mind.

As it happened, Russell got another chance to prove his worth. The coach felt the best and the fair way to go about the selection would be to let the two of them compete against each other. The stakes had been raised. As it seemed from the opinion of people, the taller of the two of them had a much better chance to win. Russell knew that he had to make his moves right this time. He needed to seize this moment in front of him. He just had to make it. He needed to perform his best. The past had shown him that big boys, older than him like his brother, could easily beat him at the game. But this time, it had to be different than what it was back then.

Both competitors were up to the task their coach put them to. Both possessed the right skill set for the position. It was about who played better than the other. The day passed. And the result was just as surprising as the events leading up to it. It was the day a modest five feet - eleven inches tall Russell won the competition against someone who was over half a foot taller than him. He had done the unbelievable. In the midst of the cheering crowd, Russell had yet to understand that there were still some people who doubted that he could play as the quarterback. And there began the skepticism about his height. Little did he know that he would have to face some harsh critics. The ones who now stood in awe of his prowess would later tell him that he was not good enough.

And there he was, the starting quarterback. He had just taken his first step towards being a pro-athlete. And it wasn't just football. Russell had been gaining attention because of his major league worthy performance at baseball too. In addition, he was also one of the star basketball players in school. He was getting closer to his dream of becoming a multi-sports star, as was the trend in his family. His father and mother couldn't have been more proud. They were happy with what he had achieved. And they always believed that Russell was built for greatness.

Chapter 5: High School Achievements

"My faith is so strong that I believe that God made me 5-11 for a reason. For all the kids that have been told, no, that they can't do it, or all the kids that will be told no."

Russell Wilson

With his leadership skills, he easily filled in the shoes of the starting quarterback. He was only beginning to experience football games that were on a level higher than what he was used to. Russell quickly became accustomed to the higher level of play and he went on to perform well in the games. He began making the local news as he led the Cougars through all-district, all-region and all-state championships. He was already the star quarterback in his first year on the team. He lead the team to the win at the State championship that year in 2004. In his junior year, he was named the Richmond Times - Dispatch player of the year. This was after he led the Cougars to another state title in 2005. Russell made the headlines with this one, and the Sports Illustrated magazine article put him in the spotlight. By the end of his junior year, he had college coaches vying for his talents. He received scholarship offers from North Carolina State University and Duke University, among others. By the start of his senior year, he had decided to play for the NC State Wolfpack football team.

His final year at high school only brought him more fame and improved Russell's game further. He was the class president that year, and he led the Cougars to win a third consecutive state title in 2006. He was named Richmond Times- Dispatch player of the year for the second year in a row. In addition to football, he was dominating the field of sports as a multi-sport star. He was remarkable with both basketball and baseball. With his performance in multiple sports, he was awarded the title of all-conference and conference player of the year.

It was no surprise that his baseball performance had teams scouting him. The Baltimore Orioles selected him in the 2007 draft. To be offered the chance to play major league baseball at such a young age delighted him. Russell was inclined to accept this offer, but he valued college education. He felt that a college education was something he would always have. He had to decline. He left for college with a promise to his father that he would graduate in three years.

Chapter 6: College and Football

"In 2007, I went to college at N.C. State because I wanted to play baseball and football. Most of all, I wanted to play quarterback in the National Football League."

Russell Wilson

Russell joined the Wolfpack in 2007 as a member of the football and baseball teams. He was a redshirt in his first season of football, although he did play as an infielder for the baseball team. The next season, he shared his starter position along with four other players. Initially, he was not coach Tom O'Brien's first choice for the position. He did not fit in the mold set for a traditional quarterback. His coach wanted him to play defensive back because he was short. Russell was already well known in the Wolfpack owing to the series of accolades he won while playing for the

Collegiate Cougars. But with his height came the disbelief that maybe he was not that good. At the training camp, the quarterbacks would be given a red jersey. But not Russell; he would mostly be given jobs to assist the quarterbacks. He longed to be given just one chance. Every day at practice, he would do his best to prove that he was up to the task. And it wasn't just sports. His inborn leadership abilities and his positive attitude were starting to show.

Wilson was always keen on getting to know people, so he fit right in with the Wolfpack. He was known as a strong person with an amazing work ethic. He was always well behaved and serious in his behavior. It was so that he was soon come to be known for his impeccable manners and his care and respect for fellow teammates. He was a good team player, but his leadership qualities were quite evident. With his rapport improving by the day, he decided to speak his mind. He went to the coach and told him he wanted to play as the quarterback. He said, "I'm going to play in the National Football League. I'm going to win multiple Super Bowls and

I'm going to be in the Hall of Fame." Coach O'Brien was taken aback. In a few days' time, he had decided, however unwillingly to give Wilson a chance.

Russell couldn't have been more excited. He knew that he wouldn't spoil this amazing opportunity that has come his way. He knew what the stakes were, and it was of the utmost importance that he prove worthy of his words. He developed steadily and he earned the position as the starting quarterback by the middle of the season. With his newfound position, he led the team to a series of wins against Duke University, the University of North Carolina and the University of Miami. In the regular season, he led the Wolfpack football team to a winning streak of four games with the team finishing at 4-3.

These wins secured NC State's entry into the Papa John's Bowl. In that game against Rutgers University, Wilson was forced to leave the game due to his picking up an injury in the third quarter. Rutgers eventually won the game even though NC State was leading the game right up to Wilson's injury. It became increasingly apparent that he was a valuable player, even though his team had lost. The Atlantic Coast Conference named him to the first team All-ACC quarterback. He was the first to be selected as a freshman to the first team.

In the 2009 season the next year, things were a bit slow for the Wolfpack. The football team lost six of eight ACC matches, allowing the opposing teams to score an upwards of 30 points in all of the matches, despite Russell's distinguished performances. He did throw 31 touchdowns in the season. He threw 252 yards per game that season, more than the 200 yards per game he averaged during his freshman year. He was declared the best quarterback in the ACC that year. He broke a few records too, including the record for the most throws without an interception.

The baseball team did poorly as well and had an overall record of 25-31 that season. Russell was unfazed and decided to work harder for the next season. The team made a comeback in 2010, where Wilson led the team to a strong 8-4 stand in the season. They then beat West Virginia in the

2010 Champs Sports Bowl by 23-7, bringing the season to a much-deserved 9-4 win. The baseball team too ended the season with 38-24 overall. Wilson also played minor league baseball that season.

This was the end of Wilson's junior year. Along with achieving at sports, he had enough credits to graduate from college. He had even earned a GPA of 4.0. He had kept the promise he made to his father. That summer, he was drafted in the fourth round by the Colorado Rockies. The next day, his father died.

Harrison had been unhealthy for quite some time; health complications from diabetes. Up until then, he had his father to guide him. All the guidance and support he had been receiving was gone. This was a big blow to Wilson, as his father's death came at a time when Russell was struggling to make a choice between baseball and football. He would spend hours on the phone with his brother. With his family to support him and his father's strong teachings of work ethic, Russell was helped out of his sadness, and he returned to the athletic field.

Chapter 7: Transfer to Wisconsin

"If I wanted to follow my dream, I had to leave N.C. State. I had no idea if I would get a second chance somewhere else."

Russell Wilson

His performance was exceptional. Wilson had become a strong contender to be selected in the NFL draft that year. Unfortunately, he received little attention from NFL scouts. They were not aware of the fact that Russell had already graduated, and knowing that college was important to him, they decided not to invite him for the 2011 NFL Scouting combine. He had free time, and he was dealing with his father's death. To keep himself occupied, he joined the Class-A minor league baseball team Asheville Tourists in the summer. He also accepted to play for the

Colorado Rockies, and he was to join the team for training that coming spring. But in his heart, he missed football.

Before his senior year started, Russell called Tom O'Brien to let him know that he would like to come back to play for the NC State football team. O'Brien has been reported to have said, "Listen, son, you're never going to play in the National Football League. You're too small. You got no shot, give it up. If you come back to NC State, you won't see the field." After a bit of negotiation, the coach offered him a spot as a substitute quarterback. But Russell was not satisfied. He knew that when he returned to NC State, he would not get another chance to play. The coach had his doubts about Russell continuing to play football since he had decided to train with a major league baseball team. In addition, he had found a new quarterback for his team, Mike Glennon.

The senior year kicked off, and with it started Russell's efforts to prove his worth yet again. He delivered his best, day after day in training. He had done the impossible numerous times in the past and he believed he could earn his place this time around too. But it was not going to happen this time. At training camp, Russell delivered his best, day after day, to no avail. Finally, the coach came up to him with an ultimatum. Wilson had to choose to quit baseball and commit to playing for the NC State football team as a quarterback or to continue to sit out the entire season.

Wilson was in a tight spot yet again. Spending a year on the bench would weaken his odds of being noticed by NFL scouts. He would miss the NFL draft, and he would have to quit football eventually. That was too much of a risk to take. The Super Bowl was his dream. He could see his hard work going down the drain. Russell started looking for ways to be able to play baseball and football at the same time. The only way he could do it was to leave NC State and transfer to another college. He had faith in himself and he knew that despite the issues with his height, he would be offered a position by other colleges. Therefore, he asked the coach to release him from his commitment with the Wolfpack. What followed was a series of controversies surrounding his transfer to a new college.

According to NCAA transfer rules, players have to redshirt for one season after switching colleges. This was something Russell had not anticipated. He ended up right where he started. He even reconsidered the original proposition that was offered to him. He was already a part of a major-league baseball team and had a near-assured chance of success. But in his heart, he wanted to play football. He had to make a choice. He would talk to his brother for hours on the phone trying to decide which road to choose. It was a difficult choice for him. Standing at the crossroads, he asked himself, "What am I capable of? Am I capable of doing what I want to do?" He could play both baseball and football really well, and it was tough to decide between almost guaranteed success and what he really wanted to achieve. Football was always his dream. He missed playing football. He had dreams of winning the Super Bowl. That was what he had prepared for his whole life. Naturally, he was inclined to choose football, but the promised glory at baseball made it confusing for him.

While Russell struggled to make his decision, things at NC State had taken yet another controversial but favorable turn. Since Russell had already graduated, he would be able to bypass sitting out the entire season after all. As it turns out, a few bylaws of the NCAA grant a waiver on the restriction on playing right after transfers to students who wish to enroll in a graduate program that is not available at their first institution. The controversy this incident caused later led the NCAA to pass a bylaw, which prevented transfers for players with only a year of eligibility remaining.

His coach finally allowed him a release from his commitment, and almost simultaneously Russell started getting offers from universities all over the United States. Russell received call after call from colleges who were interested in having him as their starting quarterback. In addition, most of them did not restrict him from playing baseball for the Rockies. In a short while, Russell had to switch from having to decide between baseball and football to exploring colleges where he could play another season. Russell would just have to enroll in a course not available for study at NC State to use the waiver. He would be, fundamentally, a hired quarterback for the new team. He already had a degree and he would have a significant amount of free time to play football. This prospect excited him and he narrowed down his options to Auburn University and the University of Wisconsin-Madison.

Both colleges needed the spot for a starting quarterback filled, and Russell was their top pick. The Wisconsin Badgers was one of the top teams with a great offensive line. Wilson visited the college, and he liked what he saw. The Auburn Tigers, on the other hand, were the defending champions. Admittedly, their line-up was not as strong as Wisconsin. After initially having found himself inclined towards going to Auburn University, he realized Wisconsin was the better option for him. Auburn had lost multiple players in the past year and was in a state of rebuilding from the ground up. Losing Wilson was a loss for the Tigers.

Chapter 8: Journey to the NFL

"Always persevere, always have a great perspective, and always have great purpose in your life"

Russell Wilson

Wilson enrolled for his masters in Educational Leadership at Wisconsin and joined the Badgers football team. Everyone on the team was incredibly welcoming towards him. He built a rapport with his teammates in no time flat and was named the team captain. That season, yet again, he raised the bar of his performance and broke numerous records. The Badgers finished the season with a record of 11 wins and 3 losses. They started off the season with a remarkable 51-17 win against the University of Nevada. They secured the top rank in the Big Ten's Leaders Division and played in the Big Ten Championship Game against

Michigan. They won it by a close 42-39 score and were to face Oregon State in the Rose Bowl in Pasadena. Unfortunately, they lost 38-45. Wilson set the single-season Football Bowl Subdivision record for passing efficiency and scored 33 passing touchdowns. He won the Griese-Brees Big Ten Quarterback of the year award. He played his final football game as quarterback for the North Team in the 2012 Nike Senior Bowl. They beat the South Team 23-13.

After what had been a thrilling season, Russell was at the top of his game. He had already been training for the NFL Scouting combine and he decided to skip the spring training with the Rockies and enter the 2012 NFL draft. Pro scouts had him in their sights, and he was predicted to be a middle-round pick by football analysts. Former NFL quarterback Chris Weinke commented, "If he was 6'5" he would probably be the No. 1 pick in the draft." His height was still an issue, but he had a strong chance of being selected in the draft.

He entered the draft as a division I-A of the FBS, the topmost level of college football, as a Big Ten

Conference player. The predictions of the analysts were accurate, and Russell could not make it in the first two rounds of the draft. In the third round, however, the Seattle Seahawks picked him. He was drafted 12th in the round and was the 75th overall pick. He was offered 3 million US dollars for a four-year contract. The Seahawks encountered a fair deal of criticism, as they had also signed another quarterback Matt Flynn, who was a free agent. Russell was named the starting quarterback after competing with Flynn. Signing him was a turning point for the Seahawks. They had only been to the Super Bowl once in their 38 year history. Russell Wilson was going to change that.

Chapter 9: Faith

"It's not about me, you know. It's not about me and it's about just helping other people."

Russell Wilson

Russell was raised in a family who believe in God as the foundation of everything in life. Russell feels grateful to God for his family and career. Belonging to a family of devout Christians, he used to go to church with his parents every Sunday. His faith was strengthened by a dream he had when he was 14. In his sleep, he saw that his father passed away and that Jesus came to his room and asked Wilson to find out more about him. The dream made Russell more serious about his faith. He has admitted that he wants to leave a legacy where he is remembered as a good Christian who lived his life in service and charity. He publicly talks about his faith and never fails to thank God in his postgame interviews. He uses his social media accounts to share verses from the Holy Bible.

From visiting the Seattle Children's Hospital on Tuesdays without fail to making a donation for every touchdown he makes, to inspiring people to have a purpose in life, Russell has shown that he cares for people. In fact, he is grateful that God has given him the opportunity to make a difference and change lives. He hosts an annual golf event to raise money for charity. His Why Not You Foundation not only provides financial support to various causes but also works to promote awareness for pediatric cancer. His foundation is also aligned with the National Domestic Violence Hotline to help put an end to domestic violence across America.

Through his hard times, Russell keeps his faith in God and credits it for being a constant support. For Russell, Jesus is someone who is always there for him. He believes his talent in sports is a gift from God. He even gives thanks to God for his height, saying,

"My faith is so strong that I believe that God made me 5-11 for a reason. For all the kids that have been told, no, that they can't do it, or all the kids that will be told no."

Chapter 10: Baseball Career

"Since I was in high school, I wanted to play professional football and professional baseball, be a two-sport star."

Russell Wilson

Texas Ranger's scout Chris Kemp recalls his first sighting of the NFL superstar Russell Wilson on a baseball field. Kemp was there to observe batting practice and he spotted the young Russell Wilson lying out in the center of the field. He was jumping up athletically against the walls to catch balls. His grandeur on the field could just not make Kemp follow the batting practice, which he had come to watch. He was so impressed with Russell's baseball skills. He remarked,

"I'd never seen anybody get after it in pregame like he did."

The intensity in practice, which Wilson displayed

during the pre-game, hinted at his dedication towards baseball and is a marker of his sportsmanship. He is a true aficionado who gives one hundred per cent, not just during the game but in the pre-game practice sessions as well.

The Denver, Colorado-based American professional baseball team, the Colorado Rockies, picked Russell Wilson in the fourth round of the year 2010 Draft. Wilson's professional American Baseball career lasted for a short one year before he made his move to the National Football League and joined the Seattle Seahawks. He played his last baseball game for Ashville of the class A South Atlantic League. Chris Kemp realized after watching Russell Wilson practice on the baseball pitch that he could be played in any position because of his athleticism. The question that then remained was whether he could bat just as well.

Russell Wilson's athleticism on the field was remarkable and he had a terrific character and temperament. He just needed to improve a little on his offensive game to achieve the same glory in major league baseball, which he achieved in football. Kemp recalls that,

"He was 89 to 90 [mph] on the mound, had good hands and, obviously, a tremendous arm..."

Wilson could have become that super utility player on the team and also be the 12th guy on the offense who could play all positions; second base, short stop and even center. Kemp was not the only scout who was impressed by Wilson's talent on the baseball field. In 2010, he was drafted by the Rockies who paid him a solid $200,000 bonus upon joining the team. Wilson later had to return a part of the bonus back to the Rockies when he gave up baseball to join the Seattle Seahawks.

The Rockies signed Russell Wilson on June 21, 2010, and officially listed him as the second baseman of the team. The Rockies were keen to utilize a lot of skills that Wilson had to offer. His athleticism and leadership quality attracted both the Seattle Seahawks as well as the Colorado Rockies. The Rockies' scouting supervisor, Jay Matthews, says that Russell was the kind of sportsman who wanted to play both football and baseball at the same time and not just play but excel at both. The Rockies drafted Wilson in the fourth round with the hope of making him a major league player once he completed 1500 minor league at-bats. Russell Wilson did not play baseball for long enough to complete 1,500 at-bats. Wilson hit .230 in 122 at-bats during the short-season Class-A Tri-City. This included two home runs and 15 RBI. The following season, Wilson batted for .228, which included three home runs and fifteen RBI in a stint of 193 at-bats. This was for Class-A Asheville after which Russell's time in Colorado came to an end.

While Russell was busy playing football, he got picked up by the Arlington-based professional baseball team, the Texas Rangers in the Rule five draft of the year 2013. Wilson has tried channeling his inner Bo Jackson by stopping by in the Ranger's training sessions occasionally. It, however, seems unlikely that he would get to star for the team unless he gives up on his NFL career with the Seahawks. It is quite difficult to pursue both the role of a quarterback as well as a professional baseball player at once. The role of the quarterback on a professional football team is pretty intense and is a position of anchor in the team, which revolves around the quarterback. Wilson in an interview to the HBO channel said, "I never want to kill the dream of playing two sports." "I would honestly play two sports."

The manager of the Rangers Jon Daniels wants Wilson to play for his team at some point in his career. Daniels clarified that by signing Wilson despite him getting drafted by the Seattle Seahawks. The Texas Rangers did not want to poach Wilson from the NFL team. They did not want to take his helmet away to replace it with a cap and a glove. Daniels remarks:

"Obviously, he's got a pretty good thing going on with the Seahawks, and we're not going to get in the way of that."

Wilson has his aspirations of becoming a multi-talented professional sports athlete still alive. Who knows what the future might hold for this talented sports star. Wilson on the Ranger's baseball team is a pretty intriguing idea.

Would the star player have managed to brush up his batting by then, or would he become a 'character guy' in the player's locker room? One thing that is for certain is that the Seahawks are glad that Russell Wilson chose to play football over baseball. For the Rangers, Wilson is a high character, winning addition to the organization.

If Russell Wilson launches his baseball career then he would be the eighth player in American sports history to have played two sports at the professional level. Players like Bo Jackson had had the privilege to play both football and baseball. Others in the list include Deion Sanders, Brian Jordan, Drew Henson and Chad Hutchinson.

During the short time in which Russell Wilson played professional baseball, he managed to hit .29 with twenty-two extra-base hits, a .356 slugging percentage and twenty-six RBIs with Class A Tri-City (2010) and Asheville (2011). The only area in which Wilson needed improvement was his swing length, a trait that could only be mastered if given enough time. Wilson instead decided to make his life-defining move over to football.

Chapter 11: Professional NFL Career

"I took a huge risk leaving baseball because I was predicted to play in the big leagues. I'm kind of a prototypical second baseman."

Russell Wilson

Ever since 2012, Russell Wilson has found just as many touchdowns as he has found himself in the spotlight of the media. His talent on the football field has been nothing short of spectacular. He is currently ranked amongst the top eight most valuable players in the NFL. He has been the most productive rookie and has quickly staggered up an impressive record at just twenty-eight years of age with the Seattle Seahawks. What makes this player tick? What makes him such a talisman with the football and on the field for the Seattle-based football team? What is the secret behind his consistency in his performance? These questions are important to decipher and can be perhaps attributed to Wilson's improvisational play throughout his career. Russell Wilson is surely no one trick pony on the field and the variations in his play make him a tricky quarterback to defend by opposing teams. More often, quarterbacks come on the scene; and have a brief spell of success until the defensive coaches in the NFL figure out their game, their strengths and their weaknesses and shut them down. This is where most of the player's effectiveness begins to wear out and gradually the player gets pushed into ignominy. This is not the case with Russell Wilson. His constantly evolving game has made him one of the toughest quarterbacks to be cracked by the opposition and has consistently helped the Seattle Seahawks become a dominant force in the National Football League.

Wilson has proved himself to be very smart in his decision making. He appears to be more confident and more comfortable in his role as a quarterback than other quarterbacks in the league. Therefore, it is no surprise that the Seahawks went on to reach two consecutive Super Bowl championship games with Russell Wilson at the helm. They won the 2013 Super Bowl by defeating the Denver Broncos 48-03. Wilson likes to shine in the most demanding of situations and his teammates surely rely a lot on his game for a win. The twenty-eight year old quarterback has proved time and again that he is one of the best in the business today.

The Seahawks offensive guard, J.R. Sweezy said that Russell Wilson simply blew him away when he showed up for the Seahawks in 2012. All the players on the team were like" Wow! How did you do that?" Sweezy believes that anytime Wilson has the ball in his hands during the game; there is a possibility of something exceptional happening on the football field for sure. It's been fifteen times in his first five years with the Seahawks that Russell Wilson has led the team to a fourth quarter or an overtime victory, coming from behind.

Amongst the many different factors that determine Russell Wilson's mettle on the football field, perhaps the most crucial one is the player's uncanny ability to outperform his opponents in crunch situations. Playing well under pressure is what many believe makes the difference between a good player and an average player. The hunger to be successful at all points in his career also sets Russell Wilson apart from other players. There is this constant desire to succeed and remain on top of his game, which makes Russell Wilson perform so well for the Seattle Seahawks. He has trained his mind to stay focused and composed in pressure situations. The role of a quarterback is perhaps the most intense role in professional football and Wilson has learned to handle the responsibility of anchoring the team brilliantly. He never seems to lose his poise and his in game decisions are truly admirable. His innate leadership qualities shine through as he leads the Seattle Seahawks to success.

Russell's versatility is evident. Many rank him as one the best game managers rather than just a quarterback due to his unconventional pocket passing ability. Russell Wilson was not a star from the first day. In fact, he had to overcome a lot of obstacles due primarily because of his rather short height for a professional quarterback. While traditionally speaking, quarterbacks are usually at least 6'4 in their height, Russell Wilson stands at a modest 5'11. This, however, has not stopped Russell from developing into one of the best quarterbacks of all time. He has broken stereotypes and has proved to the sporting world that a 5'11 man can take the football field in a storm with his exceptional sprints and surges with the ball.

Even though Russell was picked in the third round, the Seattle Seahawks felt that they were slightly pushing it and maybe could have selected him in a later round. But the manner in which Russell Wilson has played for the past five years, he has proven not just his critics wrong but history as well by becoming perhaps the best quarterback standing below six feet in the history of NFL.

There shall always be traditionalists who look for certain things in a player playing Wilson's position in a football game but the players who are actually making a difference are the ones who are consistently performing and Wilson is one of them. No matter how the player is received by the media and the historians today, the bottom line is winning games and Russell Wilson is the best at that job.

Chapter 12: Fitness

"I have high expectations of myself. I always have, always will. That will never waver. I always believe in my talent - always have."-

Russell Wilson

At this point in his career, Wilson is certainly one of the best quarterbacks playing in the NFL. Wilson's scrambling speed, throwing accuracy and throwing power makes his skill as a well-rounded quarterback hard to equal. Most of his power and strength comes from the many intense training sessions that he puts himself through at the gym. Since Russell does not possess the giant physical frame of players such as the Panthers' quarterback Cam Newton who stands at a hulking 6'5 and weighs in at 245 pounds. To overcome the physical differences he has with most other NFL quarterbacks, Russell spends extra effort and practice training his body at the gym regularly. He builds his endurance and power in order to bridge the gap between his height and frame.

Wilson works hard day in and day out mixing up his training with weights, speed exercises, Olympic lifts, sprint drills, high-intensity training exercises and German drills to ensure that he maintains his athletic shape and stamina. Here is a look at Wilson's training regimen that makes him a beast on the football field.

Russell Wilson follows a weight training program for four days out of the seven days in a week. He splits his weight lifting sessions into two speed days and two strength days. During his speed days, Wilson concentrates upon the different variants of Olympic weight lifting exercises. The speed training programs help him to develop his power which aids him in his running, cutting and scrambling.

During his strength training days of the week, Russell Wilson does some heavy lifts in order to increase his muscle power. These sessions also include corrective exercises in order to stall and avoid injuries and strains that might develop due to his heavy exercise regimen and the intense game pressure. These weight lifting sessions include dumbbells, band pull-aparts, and scap pushups. These exercises are aimed towards increasing the quarterback's upper back strength. A strong upper back is one of the first prerequisites for a successful Quarterback in NFL. This is because the quarterbacks have to endure a lot of collisions as well as make a lot of throws down the line during the game. Chiseled shoulder blades and a strong chest make it possible for Russell, and other professional quarterbacks, to maintain strength and endurance after hours of taxing pre-game training and intense game pressure.

Chapter 13: Rise to NFL Stardom

"In terms of professionally what I want to do, I want to play 15-plus more years, get to the Hall of Fame, and win a lot of championships and all that. I'd love to be the owner of a team one day. But it's way bigger than that. For me, my vision is how can I affect somebody positively every day? When you focus on other people, somehow good things happen to you. I think that's my goal. That's my vision."

Russell Wilson

At his position, Russell Wilson is one of the top five players in the NFL, which makes qualifies him as an elite player. The only other quarterbacks who might be better than Wilson at this point in their NFL careers are perhaps Tom Brady (New England Patriots) and Aaron Rodgers (Green Bay Packers). Drew Brees of the New Orleans Saints, Andrew Luck of the Indianapolis Colts and

Benjamin Todd Roethlisberger Sr. of the Pittsburgh Steelers nicknamed Big Ben are some other elite quarterbacks currently playing in the NFL. In my opinion, Wilson is the most prominent name in this list because of his records, statistics and consistency on the field. While Brees and Luck have not had great success for the past couple of seasons and Big Ben is aging fast, Wilson seems to be the future face of the NFL quarterbacks.

Wilson is just twenty-eight years of age and has made it to two consecutive Super Bowl championship games in his first three seasons as the quarterback for the Seattle Seahawks. He even managed to win one of them for his team. Perhaps the only real competition that Russell Wilson has in his professional career at this point in time is from the Carolina Panthers quarterback, Cameron Jerrell Newton. Newton is a year younger than Wilson and is also a quickly rising star, just like Russell, but Cam is much further behind Wilson in statistics due to his recent rise in performance; whereas Russell has been outshining everyone ever since his debut with the Seattle-based team in

2012.

Russell Wilson has the second-highest career passing rating in the NFL history. He stands behind Aaron Rodgers of the Green Bay Packers, Steve Young of the San Francisco 49ers and the Dallas Cowboy's former starting quarterback Tony Romo. Among all active NFL players, Russell Wilson has the highest percentage in yards per attempt and is the fourth best overall. He holds the fifth rank in completion percentage among all active NFL players and the eighth rank overall. He also has the third lowest interception rate in the history of the NFL. These impressive statistics definitely make Wilson one of the top players in the game today.

Russell Wilson is deadly accurate with his throwing capabilities. He does not take easy completion short passes and can easily work with a top flight running back while still running the offense. He is durable, enduring, quick, light on his feet and has never missed a game from injury. The only thing that can perhaps stop the young player from becoming an NFL Hall of Famer in the near future is a catastrophic injury. However, it seems that the HOF is imminent for Wilson. What sets the player apart is that Wilson seems to be improving with every game. He ups his ante after each victory and even more after a defeat. He is keen to learn, improve and progress and set to conquer every football challenge he faces. He is ruthless in his preparation and perfect in his execution. His steady and strong mindset aids him in becoming one of the greatest quarterbacks to have played in the NFL.

Watching Russell Wilson play for the Seattle Seahawks is nothing short of a treat. He has impeccable throwing capabilities. His consistency is so good that it becomes almost kind of boring. You know before every Seahawks game that Wilson is going to perform. Wilson maintains his consistency in the game by observing a strict sense of routine and order. Wilson finds his perfection through repetition. The repetition seeps into everything that the athlete does.

His consistency on the field is just as repetitive as his training routine. Consistency is difficult precisely because it is important in the game of football. The days on which Wilson is not so consistent in his game, he puts in extra hours in the next training sessions and his workout regimen to improve his strength, endurance, stamina and the leadership. The rare trait that Wilson carries in him is the ability to stay strong on the most unlikely of days, when the going is tough. The football ethics that has been ingrained in Russell Wilson is not something which he picked up during his early years in college but a deeper work ethic that he developed working with his father during his childhood.

As of 2015, Wilson finished 23 out of 32 games passing for a distance of 309 yards, which included three touchdowns. Wilson has now played twenty-five career games with multiple touchdown passes and with no interceptions. This is a record for any NFL player in the first five seasons of his career. In the six games that Russell Wilson played against AFC East opponents, he totaled a staggering record of fifteen touchdowns. Twelve out of the fifteen touchdowns were passing and three of them coming on the ground.

Russell Wilson is the first quarterback in NFL history to have a passing rating of 95.0 in each of the first three seasons of his career. His passing rating in his first three seasons with the Seattle Seahawks was 100+ for twenty-four games and that beats every other quarterback's record in the NFL. Joe Flacco of the Baltimore Ravens is tied with Wilson on the second spot along with the Cardinal's quarterback Carson Palmer who both managed the 100+ rating for nineteen games.

Wilson not only proved his passing efficiency but also became the first quarterback to have over fifteen game winning drives along with ten 4th quarter comebacks in his first three years of playing QB for the Seattle-based NFL team. This is a yet another unparalleled record. He also is one of the only five players in the history of the NFL to have made at least twenty touchdown passes in the first three seasons of their professional career in NFL.

Russell Wilson leads in the category of career

yards per passing attempt, which is 7.9. This statistic is the fourth best in the all-time records of NFL since 1951. Russell Wilson is currently ranked number one in career post-season yards per attempt. Wilson's average tallies up to be 9.01, which is the highest rating in the history of NFL. His career post-season passing rating of 97.8 is the fifth best in the all-time NFL record book.

Wilson is also the only quarterback to have more than twenty touchdown passes with ten or fewer interceptions. This is a record that Russell Wilson achieved during three seasons with the Seahawks. He also delivered seventy touchdowns in the first three seasons of his professional football career.

Chapter 14: An Unconventional Quarterback

"God's given me so much talent, and my height doesn't define my skillset. I believe that God has given me a right arm, and for some reason, even though I'm 5'11, to be able to make the throws and make great decisions on the field and all that."

Russell Wilson

Wilson had serious doubts hovering over his professional football career when he was drafted by the Seattle Seahawks in 2012. The 5'11 player did not let his short size hamper his performance and in fact, Wilson often uses his short stature to his advantage during the game. He has perfected the play-action pass that is a type of a fake handoff allowing Wilson to capitalize upon the precious time gained to scoot back behind the scrimmage line. The farther back Wilson scoots, the easier it becomes for him to spot receivers down the field.

Wilson's fake handoff technique is enhanced by his nimble footwork and his unique ability to roll out. His masterful fakes keep all the defenders at bay and from stopping him from making game winning passes. Because of this, Wilson rarely gets to take a standard three-step drop during his attempt to throw the ball over the wall of giants.

Wilson's extra-large hands, which are also very quick, allow him to tightly grip the ball while running and evading the opposition defensive line. His hands were measured at 10 ¼ inches at the scouting combine. This is the fourth highest figure in the NFL records of all times. His hands are surprisingly bigger than the hulking 6 foot seven quarterback of the Denver Broncos, Brock Osweiler.

Wilson's comparatively small size on the field gives him a very important advantage. There is not enough space to hit Wilson. According to new NFL rules, there can be no contact made below the knees. Players are also prohibited from making contact with the head of the quarterbacks. This leaves very little amount of room for Wilson to get tackled as compared to taller quarterbacks. Wilson has used this rule to his advantage by being very efficient in wriggling out of crowds and the grip of the opposition with the ball tightly tucked in his chest. When asked about the concerns of scouts and coaches regarding his height, Wilson responded by saying:

"My height's not a factor at all. My height does not define my skill set. You know where your guys are and where they're going — you just have to deliver the ball accurately and on time."

This is true as Wilson has never shown a drop in his performance which can be linked to his lack of physical attributes. He has proven to coaches and fans alike that a shorter man can also win a Super Bowl title while playing the position of the quarterback.

Chapter 15: Super Bowl XLIX Loss to Patriots

"Every day I wake up and that is my goal, to be on a constant quest for knowledge and do something different, being unique and being uncommon"

Russell Wilson

It was in the 2014 season that the Seattle Seahawks finished their regular season with a 12-4 record. This was also the season that the Seahawks made it to the Super Bowl for the second consecutive time. They had defeated the Denver Broncos in the Super Bowl the previous season and were the favorites to win yet another championship by defeating the New England Patriots.

Russell Wilson had been the hero of the crushing

victory over the Broncos. He was expected to perform well yet again and bring home the title. The game was one of the most widely viewed Super Bowl's on television. It was nothing short of a sensation. The broadcast of the game remains the most widely watched program, even today, in the network's history. The game had an average of over one hundred and fourteen million viewers. That number rose to more than one hundred and eighteen million viewers by halftime. The number further escalated to more than one hundred and twenty million viewers by the last quarter of the game, when the New England Patriots improved their performance and came from behind to defeat the Seattle Seahawks in the dying minutes of the game.

The Seahawks and the Patriots were tied at fourteen points each at halftime of the game. The game had been close and well fought between the two teams. The third quarter saw the Seattle Seahawks take a ten point lead over the Patriots. It seemed that the Seahawks were destined to win until the start of the fourth quarter. That is when the game changed and the Patriots started to take the game away from the Seahawks rapidly. The Patriots' comeback in the fourth quarter of the game is perhaps one of the most scintillating comebacks in the history of NFL Super Bowl championships. The Patriots were ruthless and not only chased down the Seahawk's ten point lead but also surpassed them in touchdowns. Seattle threatened to score in the final dying minutes of the last quarter. Wilson's throw was just a hint short of the end zone and had his pass not been intercepted by the Patriot's player, Malcolm Butler, the Seahawks would have likely won the game. Instead, the Seahawks lost a heart breaking 28 points to 24.

The loss was hard for the Seahawk's quarterback Russell Wilson who knew that his last minute pass became the game-changing interception and resulted in the Seattle Seahawk's loss to the Patriot's despite having a ten point third quarter lead. Wilson's team was trailing the Patriots 28-24 and stood facing a 2nd and goal from the one-yard line when Wilson threw the ball. This throw would haunt him for rest of his career because it prevented the Seahawks from winning their second consecutive Super Bowl.

In a video for the Player's Tribune, Wilson narrated how he suffered deeply from the loss to the Patriots and found himself responsible for the pass which got intercepted and made the Seahawks lose the game to the Patriots. But the player also opened up about how he is dealing with the disappointment.

Wilson said that moving on is most important since living in the past could start affecting his performance in the present and the future. Wilson appeared confident that he and his team could learn from the loss and that it was not just a wasted effort but also a stepping-stone to better and more historic performances by the team in the near future. The key, according to the player, is to learn and to grow. Improving your game regularly is a must in the competitive environment of American football.

In the following season, Wilson improved upon his

game; largely his passing and throwing abilities. His hunger to win every game was evident. Russell thought about his father to draw inspiration. The words of his father made him want to constantly perform better than the last time he was on field. This constantly motivated state of mind enabled Russell to lead his team to two consecutive Super Bowl title championships and make and break several NFL records.

"I remember my dad asking me one time, and it's something that has always stuck with me: 'Why not you, Russ?' You know, why not me? Why not me in the Super Bowl?"

- Russell Wilson

Chapter 16: Life and Interests

"I'm not afraid of striving to be one of the best QBs in the NFL one day. It's all about hard work."

Russell Wilson

Wilson was engaged to the singer/songwriter Ciara in March 2013. They were married on 6th July 2016. The couple chose the Peckforton Castle in Cheshire as their wedding destination. On October 2016, the couple revealed that they were expecting their first child soon.

The football star lives in Bellevue, Washington along with Ciara and their two great Danes.

Russell Wilson is a regular social contributor in the Seattle community. During the season, Wilson on his weekly day off, makes it a point to visit the Seattle Children's Hospital. He also visits soldiers at Joint Base Lewis-McChord. Wilson also hosts a youth training football camp every year in different cities. This is very important for the player because he believes that talent should be developed from a young age. Providing children who love the game with state of the art training and facilities along with professional insight into the game is Wilson's effort to promote the football culture in the United States. The proceeds from the Russell Wilson Passing Academy went to support of the Charles Ray III Diabetes Association. Wilson also happens to be the ambassador of this organization. Russell Wilson, in the years 2013 and 2014, entered into "invested with Russell" program by partnering with Russell Investments. This program donated three thousand dollars to Wilson's charitable foundation for every touchdown that the player scored during a game.

Conclusion

I would like to thank all the readers for taking out of their precious time to purchase and read this book on the life of one of the most popular quarterbacks playing American football today. Russell Wilson came from a family that promoted the sporting ethos and culture. He was initiated into the NFL swiftly after being drafted by the Seattle Seahawks in the year 2012.

Ever since then, the talented athlete has not looked back. He has been gaining experience and improving his abilities from one season to the next. He is perhaps one of the best quarterbacks playing in the NFL today.

Russell Wilson has stacked up an impressive record as well in the short five years since he has being playing professional football. He never let his unconventional physique impede his game in any way. He works extra hard while training to put in more than 100% during the game. We can learn much from studying Russell Wilson's work ethic and will power.

Thank you once again for reading this book. I hope this has been an informative and an enjoyable experience for you.

Made in the USA
Las Vegas, NV
12 December 2020

12923039R00046